Major European Union Nations

CARDIFF
CAERDYDD

Major
European Union
Nations

Austria	Italy
Belgium	The Netherlands
Czech Republic	Poland
Denmark	Portugal
France	Spain
Germany	Sweden
Greece	United Kingdom
Ireland	

Major European
Union Nations

BELGIUM

Ida Walker and Shaina C. Indovino

Mason Crest

Mason Crest
370 Reed Road, Broomall,
Pennsylvania 19008
www.masoncrest.com

Printed in the Hashemite Kingdom of Jordan.

First printing
9 8 7 6 5 4 3 2 1

Library of Congress Cataloging-in-Publication Data

Walker, Ida.
  Belgium / by Ida Walker and Shaina C. Indovino.
      p. cm. — (The European Union : political, social, and economic cooperation)
  Includes bibliographical references and index.
  ISBN 978-1-4222-2233-1 (hardcover) — ISBN 978-1-4222-2231-7 (series hardcover) — ISBN 978-1-4222-9263-1 (ebook)
  1. Belgium—Juvenile literature. 2. European Union—Belgium—Juvenile literature. I. Indovino, Shaina Carmel. II. Title.
  DH418.W35 2012
  949.304'4—dc22
                              2010051078

Produced by Harding House Publishing Services, Inc.
www.hardinghousepages.com
Interior design by Benjamin Stewart.
Cover design by Torque Advertising + Design.

CONTENTS

BELGIUM

European Union Member since 1952

Knokke

Oostende

⊙Brugge

Turnhout

⊙Antwerp

Sint-Niklaas

Herentals

⊙Ghent

Dendermonde

Mechelen

Aarschot

Roeselare

⊙Hasselt

Kortrijk

Leuven

☆Brussels

Mouscron

Ronse

Tienen   Sint-Truiden

Halle

Wavre

Tournai Leuze Ath

⊙Liége

Soignies

Verviers

Huy

Spa

Mons

Namur

Malmédy

Charleroi

Dinant

Marche-en-Famenne

Philippeville

Chimay

Bastogne

Neufchâteau

Bouillon

Arlon⊙

INTRODUCTION

Sixty years ago, Europe lay scarred from the battles of the Second World War. During the next several years, a plan began to take shape that would unite the countries of the European continent so that future wars would be inconceivable. On May 9, 1950, French Foreign Minister Robert Schuman issued a declaration calling on France, Germany, and other European countries to pool together their coal and steel production as "the first concrete foundation of a European federation." "Europe Day" is celebrated each year on May 9 to commemorate the beginning of the European Union (EU).

The EU consists of twenty-seven countries, spanning the continent from Ireland in the west to the border of Russia in the east. Eight of the ten most recently admitted EU member states are former communist regimes that were behind the Iron Curtain for most of the latter half of the twentieth century.

Any European country with a democratic government, a functioning market economy, respect for fundamental rights, and a government capable of implementing EU laws and policies may apply for membership. Bulgaria and Romania joined the EU in 2007. Croatia, Serbia, Turkey, Iceland, Montenegro, and Macedonia have also embarked on the road to EU membership.

While the EU began as an idea to ensure peace in Europe through interconnected economies, it has evolved into so much more today:

- Citizens can travel freely throughout most of the EU without carrying a passport and without stopping for border checks.

- EU citizens can live, work, study, and retire in another EU country if they wish.

- The euro, the single currency accepted throughout seventeen of the EU countries (with more to come), is one of the EU's most tangible achievements, facilitating commerce and making possible a single financial market that benefits both individuals and businesses.

- The EU ensures cooperation in the fight against cross-border crime and terrorism.

- The EU is spearheading world efforts to preserve the environment.

- As the world's largest trading bloc, the EU uses its influence to promote fair rules for world trade, ensuring that globalization also benefits the poorest countries.

- The EU is already the world's largest donor of humanitarian aid and development assistance, providing around 60 percent of global official development assistance to developing countries in 2011.

The EU is not a nation intended to replace existing nations. The EU is unique—its member countries have established common institutions to which they delegate some of their sovereignty so that decisions on matters of joint interest can be made democratically at the European level.

Europe is a continent with many different traditions and languages, but with shared values such as democracy, freedom, and social justice, cherished values well known to North Americans. Indeed, the EU motto is "United in Diversity."

Enjoy your reading. Take advantage of this chance to learn more about Europe and the EU!

Ambassador John Bruton,
Former EU President and Prime Minister of Ireland

1 MODERN ISSUES

Belgium is a unique member of the European Union. In addition to being one of the six original founding members of what would later become the EU, Belgium is home to one of the EU's official seats. Brussels, a large city located right in the center of Belgium, has historically been the home of the European Commission.

Although there are no officially declared capitals of Europe, many Belgians refer to Brussels as the capital of the EU because of its history and importance. France and Luxembourg have felt the same way about their own cities, Strasbourg and Luxembourg. However, according to unbiased opinion, Brussels is generally considered to be one of three capitals of the European Union, sharing the title with Strasbourg and Luxembourg equally.

Ever since the European Union was formed, Belgium has always been one of its strongest supporters. Leading Belgian politicians have also played key roles in the EU, and Belgium's identi-

BELGIUM AND NATO

Brussels is also the headquarters of NATO, the North Atlantic Treaty Organization. Unlike the EU, member states of NATO are not only from Europe. The United States, for instance, has been a member of NATO since its beginning. In fact, the North Atlantic Treaty that brought NATO into existence was signed in Washington, D.C. in 1949! Although the EU and NATO are very different organizations, their aims are very similar—peace, security, and fairness for all.

ty has long been shaped by the country's membership in the European Community. The EU plays an important role in Belgians' daily lives.

THE ROMA

For more than a thousand years, the Roma—sometimes known as Gypsies—have been an important part of European civilization. Today, with an estimated population of 10 to 12 million people, Roma are the biggest ethnic minority in Europe. They live in all countries within the EU, and most are EU citizens.

Despite this, the Roma in Europe often face racism and poor living conditions. Their children have fewer educational opportunities, and their housing is often unhealthy and unsafe. People often treat them cruelly, and many employers are reluctant to hire them.

The EU is officially committed to improving the Roma's situation. Despite that, world leaders have criticized the Belgian President of the Council of the European Union (whose term ended December 31, 2010) for not doing enough for the Roma. Instead, he virtually ignored the issue. In his assessment report of the Belgian presidency posted on the presidency website, he did not even mention the word "Roma," despite the fact that the year 2010 was dedicated as the "European Year for Combating Poverty and Social Exclusion."

Roma children have fewer educational oppurtunities than the rest of the population, and often live out their lives in poverty.

Offices of the European Union.

The Formation of the European Union (EU)

The EU is a confederation of European nations that continues to grow. As of 2012, there are twenty-seven official members. Several other candidates are also waiting for approval. All countries that enter the EU agree to follow common laws about foreign security policies. They also agree to cooperate on legal matters that go on within the EU. The European Council meets to discuss all international matters and make decisions about them. Each country's own concerns and interests are important, though. And apart from legal and financial issues, the EU tries to uphold values such as peace, human dignity, freedom, and equality.

All member countries remain autonomous. This means that they generally keep their own laws and regulations. The EU becomes involved only if there is an international issue or if a member country has violated the principles of the union.

The idea for a union among European nations was first mentioned after World War II. The war had devastated much of Europe, both physically and financially. In 1950, the French foreign minister suggested that France and West Germany combine their coal and steel industries under one authority. Both countries would have control over the industries. This would help them become more financially stable. It would also make war between the countries much more difficult. The idea was interesting to other European countries as well. In 1951, France, West Germany, Belgium, Luxembourg, the Netherlands, and Italy signed the Treaty of Paris, creating the European Coal and Steel Community. These six countries would become core of the EU.

In 1957, these same countries signed the Treaties of Rome, creating the European Economic Community. In 1965, the Merger Treaty formed the European Community. Finally, in 1992, the Maastricht Treaty was signed. This treaty defined the European Union. It gave a framework for expanding the EU's political role, particularly in the area of foreign and security policy. It would also replace national currencies with the euro. The next year, the treaty went into effect. At that time, the member countries included the original six plus another six who had joined during the 1970s and '80s.

In the following years, the EU would take more steps to form a single market for its members. This would make joining the union even more of an advantage. Three more countries joined during the 1990s. Another twelve joined in the first decade of the twenty-first century. As of 2012, six countries were waiting to join the EU.

Muslim children praying.

Muslims in Belgium

Another group of people who face discrimination in Belgium and the rest of the EU are Muslims. Islam (the religion Muslims practice) is the largest minority religion in Belgium, and a 2008 estimation found that 6 percent of the Belgian population (about 628,751 people) is Muslim. The Belgium government officially recognized Islam in the early 1970s, and in 2006, the government gave $7.7 million (6.1 million euros) to Islamic groups. But many Belgians are not happy about the presence of Muslims in their country, and according to a 2006 opinion poll, 61 percent of the Belgian population thinks tensions between Muslims and other Belgians will get still worse in the future.

Some Muslims have been connected with terrorist incidents in Belgium, which has increased this tension. On the other side of the story, several Belgian communities have passed laws against women appearing in public wearing the traditional Muslim head covering. Under a 1993 executive order, persons in the streets must be identifiable, based on laws dating back to the Middle Ages. A veil that does not completely cover the

How Does Presidency of the Council of the EU work?

To ensure fairness among all members of the European Union, member states take turns sharing presidency of the council. The title of "president" is not held by just one person, but rather the national government. Starting in 2007, the idea of presidency trios was introduced. This means that three separate countries share the title of president, switching every six months. However, these trios work closely with one another to ensure that the agendas put in place by one president will be continued by the others. This means that more can get done in a shorter period of time because every president in the year and a half-long period of one trio will be working toward common goals.

face is allowed, but in a few cases, women have been fined $190 (150 euros) for ignoring the ban.

Environmental Issues

Cities cover most of Belgium. This means the amount of pollution created by the entire nation has the potential to be particularly high for a country of its size. Wallonia, in southern Belgium, is finding it difficult to switch from the old ways of coal and steel to the new industries more common in the north. This is one of the many reasons the secession of Flanders from Belgium would be economically devastating to Wallonia. However,

Muslim woman in Belgium can be fined for wearing their traditional head coverings, which prevent their faces from being seen.

MUSLIMS IN THE EUROPEAN UNION

Muslims are people who follow Islam, a religion that grew from some of the same roots as Judaism and Christianity. "Islam" means "submission to God," and Muslims try to let God shape all aspects of their lives. They refer to God as Allah; their holy scriptures are called the Qur'an, and they consider the Prophet Muhammad to be their greatest teacher.

About 16 million Muslims live in the European Union—but their stories vary from country to country. Some Muslim populations have been living in Europe for hundreds of years. Others came in the middle of the twentieth century. Still others are recent refugees from the troubled Middle East. By 2020, the Muslim population in Europe is predicted to double. By 2050, one in five Europeans are likely to be Muslim, and by 2100, Muslims may make up one-quarter of Europe's people.

Not all Europeans are happy about these predictions. Negative stereotypes about Muslims are common in many EU countries. Some Europeans think all Muslims are terrorists. But stereotypes are dangerous!

When you believe a stereotype, you think that people in a certain group all act a certain way. "All jocks are dumb" is a stereotype. "All women are emotional" is another stereotype, and another is, "All little boys are rough and noisy." Stereotypes aren't true! And when we use stereotypes to think about others, we often fall into prejudice—thinking that some groups of people aren't as good as others.

Fundamentalist Muslims want to get back to the fundamentals—the basics—of Islam. However, their definition of what's "fundamental" is not always the same as other Muslims'. Generally speaking, they are afraid that the influence of Western morals and values will be bad for Muslims. They believe that the laws of Islam's holy books should be followed literally. Sometimes, they are willing to kill for their beliefs—and they are often willing to die for them as well. Men and women who are passionate about these beliefs have taken part in violent attacks against Europe and the United States. They believe that terrorism will make the world take notice of them, that it will help them fight back against the West's power.

But most Muslims are not terrorists. In fact, most Muslims are law-abiding and hardworking citizens of the countries where they live. Some Muslims, however, believe that women should have few of the rights that women expect in most countries of the EU. This difference creates tension, since the EU guarantees women the same rights as men.

But not all Muslims are so conservative and strict. Many of them believe in the same "golden rule" preached by all major religions: "Treat everyone the way you want to be treated."

But despite this, hate crimes against Muslims are increasing across the EU. These crimes range from death threats and murder to more minor assaults, such as spitting and name-calling. Racism against Muslims is a major problem in many parts of the EU. The people of the European Union must come to terms with the fact that Muslims are a part of them now. Terrorism is the enemy to be fought—not Muslims.

Over 50 percent of Belgium's electricity is produced by nuclear power.

Wallonia is making a slow and steady shift to cleaner industries. Hopefully, it will catch up to the northern regions soon.

Belgium is also focusing on the forms of energy it uses in an effort to reduce the amount of environmental impact it has. Unfortunately, Belgium is far behind most countries in the EU, with over 50 percent of electricity generated through nuclear power alone. Gas power accounts for another 30 percent, and renewable energy sources account for, at most, an approximate 3 percent of all energy. The amount of pollution in Belgium is also particularly high because of its geographic location, right in the center of Europe.

POLITICAL ISSUES

Politics in Belgium are a lot more complicated than in the United States! Because of its geographic location and history, Belgium has three official spoken languages. Most citizens speak either Dutch or French, but a large number of them speak German, making it Belgium's third official language. Because of this, people choose their political parties based both on their ideals and on the language they speak. It's all very complicated, especially since there are currently twelve political parties represented in Belgium. Compare that to the much smaller number we see in the United States!

In recent years, political power has shifted greatly. In the 2010 elections, the two most rep-

resented parties were the New Flemish Alliance and the Socialist Party. The New Flemish Alliance is a **right-wing** political party, and the largest Dutch-speaking one. The Socialist Party is the largest French-speaking party.

Belgium has a very long history in which portions of it were part of several different countries, including the Netherlands and France. The existence of so many political parties is a direct result of Belgium's past; instead of being based on political ideals alone, political parties are created with the intention of protecting the interests of a particular culture and population.

Belgium's history and cultural diversity, in addition to the clear division of spoken language, have led to a lot of inner turmoil. While some believe these two culturally diverse regions should be separated, others believe they should stay together. The term "separatist" has been used to describe people who are in favor of separation. Some political parties want Flanders to **secede** from Belgium. (Flanders is the name of the Dutch-speaking area in the northern Belgium, and Wallonia is the name of the southern, French-speaking part of Belgium.)

The discussion has been going on for decades and there is no answer in sight. Many who were against the split between Flanders and Wallonia believed the cost of independence would destroy the economies of the newly separated countries. However, those in favor of separation continue to raise their voices.

The city of Tournai

2
CHAPTER

BELGIUM'S HISTORY AND GOVERNMENT

Belgium has played an important part in Europe's history. Strategically located between Europe and England, empires wrestled for control of its trade routes and industries.

The Kingdom of Belgium, as we know it today, came into existence in 1830. Until then, it was a part of the United Kingdom of the Netherlands. Belgium won its independence from

Today this area is made up of France, Belgium, western Switzerland, and parts of the Netherlands.

Belgium derives its name from a **Celtic** tribe, the Belgae, whom Julius Caesar described as the most courageous tribe of Gaul. However, the Belgae were forced to yield to Roman legions during the first century BCE. For the next three hundred years, the region that is now Belgium flourished as a province of Rome.

After the collapse of the Roman Empire in 406 CE, the Franks invaded the region. The Franks were a loose **confederation** of Germanic tribes who had been pushed out of Germany by Attila the Hun. Under the Franks, Christianity spread, and churches and monasteries were built across the entire region.

DATING SYSTEMS AND THEIR MEANING

You might be accustomed to seeing dates expressed with the abbreviations BC or AD, as in the year 1000 BC or the year AD 1900. For centuries, this dating system has been the most common in the Western world. However, since BC and AD are based on Christianity (BC stands for Before Christ and AD stands for *anno Domini*, Latin for "in the year of our Lord"), many people now prefer to use abbreviations that people from all religions can be comfortable using. The abbreviations BCE (meaning Before Common Era) and CE (meaning Common Era), mark time in the same way (for example, 1000 BC is the same year as 1000 BCE, and AD 1900 is the same year as 1900 CE), but BCE and CE do not have the same religious overtones as BC and AD.

the Dutch as a result of an uprising of the Belgian people. A **constitutional monarchy** was established in 1831, and Leopold of Saxe-Coburg was appointed king of Belgium.

CELTIC ROOTS

Belgium's recorded history can be traced back about two thousand years. Belgium was then part of a much larger region the Romans called Gaul. Gaul comprised the entire west European region.

CHARLEMAGNE: HOLY ROMAN EMPEROR

Under the rule of Emperor Charlemagne, the Frankish Empire extended from the Elbe to the Atlantic, and from the North Sea to the Mediterranean. As a result, in 800 CE, the pope himself crowned Charlemagne as the first Holy Roman Emperor. After his death, the empire was divided between his sons.

karolus impant

magnus Annis 14

A portrait of Charlemagne by the artist Durer

THE RISE OF FLANDERS

The fall of the Frankish Empire created a power vacuum. Baldwin the Iron Arm from Flanders profited from the weakness of the French throne to become a strong leader. From the twelfth century onward, the blossoming of trade between the Continent (continental Europe) and England resulted in the rapid growth of the cities in Flanders.

Brugge became the trading center for goods from Italy, France, Germany, and England. The growing textile industry was also a vital factor in the increasing wealth and prestige of the cities, although this industry relied on a steady supply of wool from England.

The Hundred Years' War between France and England began in 1337. Flanders sided with the French against England, causing England to **boycott** the delivery of wool to the region. Trade in Flanders came to a complete halt. To get the economy back on its feet, merchants and craftsmen rebelled against their rulers to reestablish trade with England. Trade blossomed once again, bringing back old conflicts of interests between merchants and craftsmen. As matters came to a boil, a full-fledged **civil war** robbed Flanders of all power it had gained.

GOLDEN AGE OF THE BURGUNDIANS

In the early fifteenth century, Philip, the duke of Burgundy, married the daughter and heiress of the count of Flanders. After the count's death, Belgian Flanders, Artois, and other territories were incorporated into the Burgundian **duchy**. The Burgundian household now controlled an area comprising today's Netherlands and Belgium.

The Burgundian era was a tense period of history. But amid the ravages of war, the art world of Flanders flourished.

BELGIUM UNDER SPANISH RULE

In 1477, Marie of Burgundy married Austrian ruler Maximilian, a member of the Hapsburg family. Maximilian's grandson inherited the Spanish crown (and eventually the crown of Holy Roman Emperor), bringing Belgium under Spanish influence. This ignited a long battle against Catholic Spanish rule.

During the sixteenth century, Dutch-speaking parts of the Netherlands became Protestant, while the southern, Flemish parts remained Roman Catholic. The Catholic king of Spain, Philip II, strictly **suppressed** Protestantism during the mid-sixteenth century, especially in Flanders. Thousands were imprisoned or executed before full-scale war erupted in 1568. The Revolt of the Netherlands lasted eighty years, and in the end, Protestant Holland and its allied provinces booted out the Spaniards. The dominantly Catholic areas of Belgium and Luxembourg stayed under Spanish rule.

An example of fifteenth-century Flanders art.

AUSTRIA TAKES OVER

The death of Charles II, the last of the Spanish Habsburgs, effectively ended Spanish rule of Belgium. In the ensuing power struggle, Belgium passed into Austria's hands.

Belgium experienced enormous economic prosperity under the Austrian queen Maria Theresa. Trade and industry grew. Roads were built, linking important cities such as Brussels and Vienna. Arts and crafts also reached their *zenith*. Tournai was a manufacturing center for porcelain. The fashion for lace reached its peak, and architecture flourished.

TOSSED BETWEEN NATIONS

Toward the latter part of the eighteenth century, revolts broke out across Belgium, leading to the formation of the United States of Belgium, a loose **conglomeration** of **sovereign** states. In 1794, the troops of the new Austrian emperor, Leopold II, forcibly brought Belgium back into the Austrian fold.

The following year, during the Austrian and Prussian war against Revolutionary France, Napoleonic France beat the Austrian army. France occupied both Belgium and the Netherlands, which were combined and renamed the Batavian Republic. Belgium remained under French dominion for the next twenty years.

With the defeat of Napoleon's army at the Battle of Waterloo, fought just a few miles south of Brussels, Belgium was separated from France. In 1815, the Congress of Vienna made Belgium part of the Netherlands. The new United Kingdom of the Netherlands was ruled by the Dutch House of Orange.

In 1830, Belgium won its independence from the Dutch as a result of an uprising of the Belgian people. The French-speaking minority controlled the factories and other economic resources. They did not want to live under a Dutch-speaking administration, and they mounted a revolution. The fact that Belgium was mostly Catholic and the Netherlands predominantly Protestant also played a role.

A constitutional monarchy was established in 1831. King Leopold I from the House of Saxe-Coburg in Germany was invited to be monarch. To celebrate Belgium's hard-won freedom, July 21 was proclaimed a day of national rejoicing.

BELGIUM AND COLONIALISM

In 1865, Leopold II became king. His first act as king was to satisfy his **colonial** ambitions. Through a policy of murder, deception, and colonialism, Leopold gained control of the entire Congo basin in Africa. He made the land his private property and called it the Congo Free State. Here the local population was brutalized in exchange for rubber.

In 1908, under international pressure, Leopold II was forced to give his property to the Belgian state as a colony. From then onward, it became the Belgian Congo until it gained its independence from Belgium in 1960.

WORLD WAR I

Belgium was one of the bloodiest battlegrounds of World War I. The area around Ypres witnessed some of the worst fighting of the entire war, with huge loss of life on both sides. For the first time in war, poison gas was used—first chlorine gas in 1915 and then mustard gas in 1917.

Although Germany defeated Belgium, after the war, Belgium was able to regain its territories, as well as additional German-speaking regions in Eupen-Malmedy. It was also given the former German colonies of Rwanda and Burundi in Africa.

Belgium's devastation after World War II

The Belgian parliament meets in the buildings around Grand-Place, Brussel's Central Square.

WORLD WAR II

To counter Germany's continued aggression after World War I, Belgium's King Albert I declared his nation a **neutral** country in 1936. His declaration did little good. On May 10, 1940, German troops invaded Belgium. As the Nazi forces scoured Belgium for Jews, the Belgian spirit rose to the occasion. Many Belgians showed great courage in their commitment to aid the persecuted and become active in the **Resistance**.

But by the time the Allied forces freed the last Belgian city in 1945, Belgium was in ruins. The task of rebuilding the cities and nations now lay ahead.

EUROPEAN UNION—BELGIUM

BUILDING PARTNERSHIPS

The German invasions during the two world wars made Belgium one of the foremost advocates of **collective security** within the framework of European **integration** and the Atlantic partnership.

In 1948, the customs and economic union BENELUX (Belgium, the Netherlands, and Luxembourg) was formed. These countries, along with France, West Germany, and Italy, formed the European Coal and Steel Community (ECSC) "to substitute for age-old rivalries the merging of essential interest." In 1957, the same countries signed the Treaty of Rome, which established the European Economic Community (EEC), now known as the European Union or the EU.

REBUILDING BELGIUM

Compared to its neighboring countries, Belgium's economic recovery after the world wars was rapid. The harbor of Antwerp had been spared major damage during the conflict, and the country's energy reserves were adequate to supply all the necessary power.

In May 1945, **exiled** King Leopold III returned to Belgium to hostile citizens. After fierce protests between groups that supported him and those who wanted the monarchy abolished, Leopold **abdicated** in favor of his son Baudouin I. Economic prosperity followed the change in leadership. So did a formal language border in 1962.

BELGIUM TODAY

Since 1970, three communities and three regions have existed within Belgium: the Flemish, the French- and the German-speaking communities; and the Flemish, the Walloon, and the Brussels regions.

In 1980, measures were taken to expand the authority of the regions, which were granted their own rights and institutions. Today, although Belgium is a constitutional monarchy with a **parliamentary** form of government, the country has a complex system of municipalities, provinces, and regions as well as a centralized state.

The central state has authority in national defense, foreign affairs, social issues, agriculture, justice, and financial and monetary issues. Policymaking areas such as the economy, education, transport, and the environment have all been passed on to the regions.

In 1993, King Baudouin's brother, Albert II, took over the throne. After his ascension, Belgium reformed the **bicameral** parliamentary system and provided for the direct election of the members of community and regional legislative councils.

Despite its outward calm, Belgium remains a surprisingly **volatile** country. From 2010 until the end of 2011, Belgium's government was deadlocked between two parties. Finally, in December 2011, a new socialist prime minister was sworn in, ending the long stalemate between political parties.

The Belgian city of Ghent

3 THE ECONOMY

By keeping its doors open to people, goods, and services from all over the globe, Belgium has made its citizens among the richest in the world. This relatively small country has few natural resources, limited land, and a population of just over ten million, yet by focusing on its

Quick Facts: The Economy of Belgium

Gross Domestic Product (GDP): US$412 billion (2011 est.)

GDP per capita: US$37,600 (2011 est.)

Industries: engineering and metal products, motor vehicle assembly, transportation equipment, scientific instruments, processed food and beverages, chemicals, basic metals, textiles, glass, petroleum

Agriculture: sugar beets, fresh vegetables, fruits, grain, tobacco; beef, veal, pork, milk

Export Commodities: machinery and equipment, chemicals, finished diamonds, metals and metal products, foodstuffs

Export Partners: Germany 19.1%, France 17%, Netherlands 12.2%, UK 7.2%, US 5.3%, Italy 4.7% (2010)

Import Commodities: raw materials, machinery and equipment, chemicals, raw diamonds, pharmaceuticals, foodstuffs, transportation equipment, oil products

Import Partners: Netherlands 19.1%, Germany 16.4%, France 11.3%, UK 5.4%, US 5.3%, Ireland 5.3%, China 4.1% (2010)

Currency: euro (EUR)

Currency Exchange Rate: US $1= 0.7107 (March, 2011)

Note: All figures are from 2011 unless otherwise noted.
Source: www.cia.gov, 2012.

strengths—skills in metalworking, a strong base in heavy industry, an extensive transportation network, and easy access to international trade routes—Belgium has become the financial center of Europe.

Today, the biggest companies, the most important institutions of the EU, nearly fifty intergovernmental agencies, and NATO headquarters are located in Brussels, Belgium's capital city. No wonder that one-third of the city's population is foreign, mainly European.

Belgium conducts nearly three-fourths of its trade with EU member states, predominantly neighboring countries such as France, Germany, and the Netherlands. A first-tier member of the European Monetary Union, Belgium shifted away from the use of the Belgium franc (BF) to the use of the euro as its currency after January 1, 2002.

Industry

By making good use of its skills in metalworking and heavy industry, Belgium has created an industrial base that accounts for 25 percent of the country's *gross domestic product (GDP)*. Most of Belgium's industrial plants are located in the Flanders region, in the corridor between Antwerp and Brussels.

Industries such as steel, chemicals, shipbuilding, automobiles, glass, paper, food processing, and heavy machinery employ one-fifth of the Belgian workforce. Belgium's crude petroleum, most of which is imported, is processed in *refineries* located in Antwerp. Some of the biggest, brightest,

Refineries in Antwerp process crude petroleum imported from other countries.

and most expensive diamonds in the world are cut and sold in Antwerp. Belgium is also one of the world's leading processors of cobalt, radium, copper, zinc, and lead, all of which are imported in their raw form.

Foreign investment in Belgium brought with it a boom in the country's engineering sector in the late twentieth century. The country has assembly plants for American, Swedish, German, and French automobiles, including Ford, Volvo, Opel, and Volkswagen. Most of these cars are imported to the European market.

Belgium is also home to large multinational corporations manufacturing heavy electrical motors, machine tools, specialized plastics, chemicals, and pharmaceuticals.

The Brussels airport connects Belgium to the world.

SERVICES

Throughout history, Belgium has offered the world a convenient place to conduct business. Located at the crossroads of Europe, Belgium is a takeoff point for trade and traffic between Europe and the Americas.

Large **service industries** from all over the world have taken advantage of Belgium's location.

Banking, information technology, insurance, recruitment, travel, and tourism account for 71 percent of the Belgian economy and employ two-thirds of the Belgian workforce. Thousands of Belgians

are also employed by the many EU, NATO, and other intergovernmental offices based in Brussels.

In the banking sector, the Société Générale de Belgique dominates the market. The Savings Bank of the General Savings and Pensions Fund is the major financial organization for the collection of savings. The National Bank is charged with issuing currency and has considerable **autonomy**.

Belgium has also become a tourist's paradise. More than six million tourists visit each year, attracted to historical towns such as Brussels, Brugge, Ghent, and Liège, as well as seaside resorts such as Spa, Knokke, Ostend, and Dinant. In the south, the wooded region of the Ardennes is popular with nature lovers and hikers.

TRANSPORT

Belgium's transportation facilities—railways, waterways, airways, and roadways—are all well developed.

With one mile of railroad track for every 1.4 miles of land, the country has one of the densest railway networks in the world. Brussels is the hub of a series of railroad lines that radiate outward, like the spokes of a wheel, and link the capital to other cities both inside and outside the country.

Belgium also has an extensive network of inland waterways. Canals connect cities such as Brugge and Ghent to the North Sea. Belgium's two main rivers, the Schelde and the Meuse, are the economic lifelines of Flanders and Wallonia, respectively. Antwerp, on the Schelde River, is the country's chief port.

The Brussels Airport is the center of international Belgian air traffic. Smaller international facilities are maintained at Antwerp, Liège, Charleroi, and Ostend. Sabena, the national airline, flies both internationally and domestically.

As for roadways, most of Belgium's roads are paved and of high quality. Cars and bicycles often share the roads.

ELECTRICITY

Nearly 60 percent of Belgium's electricity comes from its nuclear plants. **Thermal** power plants, using imported coal, generate 38 percent of Belgium's power. Less than 1 percent of Belgium's electricity is generated in its **hydroelectric** power plants.

AGRICULTURE, FISHING, AND FORESTRY

Agriculture contributes just 0.7 percent to the Belgian economy. Nearly one-fifth of Belgium's agricultural land consists of pastures and meadows. Cattle raising and breeding and the production of milk are the main agricultural activities.

Belgian farms are highly **mechanized**. The average yields of wheat, sugar beets, potatoes, and milk are among the highest in the world. Major crops include sugar beets, potatoes, wheat, barley, apples, tomatoes, oats, corn (maize), chicory (endive), and **flax**. The growing of flowers, ornamental plants, and flower bulbs is a rising industry in the Flanders region.

Belgium is famous for its chocolate.

Belgium's small fishing industry is based in the coastal towns of Zeebrugge and Ostend along the North Sea. All products of the fishing industry are used within the country itself.

The planted forests of the Ardennes and the Kempenland support Belgium's relatively small forest-products industry. Mechanization has helped growth in the forest industry, allowing Belgium to reduce its reliance on imported timber.

NATURAL RESOURCES

COAL AND METALLIC ORES

Belgium's most important mineral resources, coal and metallic ores, have been **depleted**. The coal needs of the steel industry, thermal power plants, and domestic heating are met through imports. Belgium also imports large quantities of iron ore and zinc, since the refining of metallic ores is an important component of Belgium's economy.

CHALK, LIMESTONE, SAND, CLAY, AND MARBLE

The mining of chalk and limestone supports a significant cement industry in Wallonia. Sand is mined in the Kempenland for use in glass manufacturing. In Borinage, clay is mined for pottery products and bricks. Stones, mostly marbles, also are quarried.

WATER

Belgium has plenty of water, but most of it is concentrated in the southern part of the country in the form of streams and groundwater. However, most of Belgium's population lives in the north. To meet the country's needs, Belgium has elaborate water-transfer systems involving canals, storage basins, and pipelines. Today, the key problem facing Belgium is water pollution caused largely by industries located along Belgium's main rivers.

TRIMMING THE ECONOMY

As a member of the EU, Belgium needed to streamline its economy, reduce its debt, and balance its account books. These are especially important measures considering the current economic downturn. Belgium has struggled in the last few years to keep its economy healthy.

The social security system, which expanded rapidly during the prosperous 1950s and 1960s, includes pensions, a medical system, unemployment insurance coverage, child allowances, and invalid benefits. The economic decline of the 1970s found the system facing an increasing burden and accounted for much of the government budget **deficits**.

In response to EU guidelines, Belgium restructured major industries and introduced **austerity** measures in public spending. Today, inflation in Belgium is at 2.3 percent (2010 estimate), and government debt is on the high end, since the national deficit was 3.8% of GDP in 2011, above the EU guidelines.

The Mont des Arts gardens in Brussels provides a romantic meeting place.

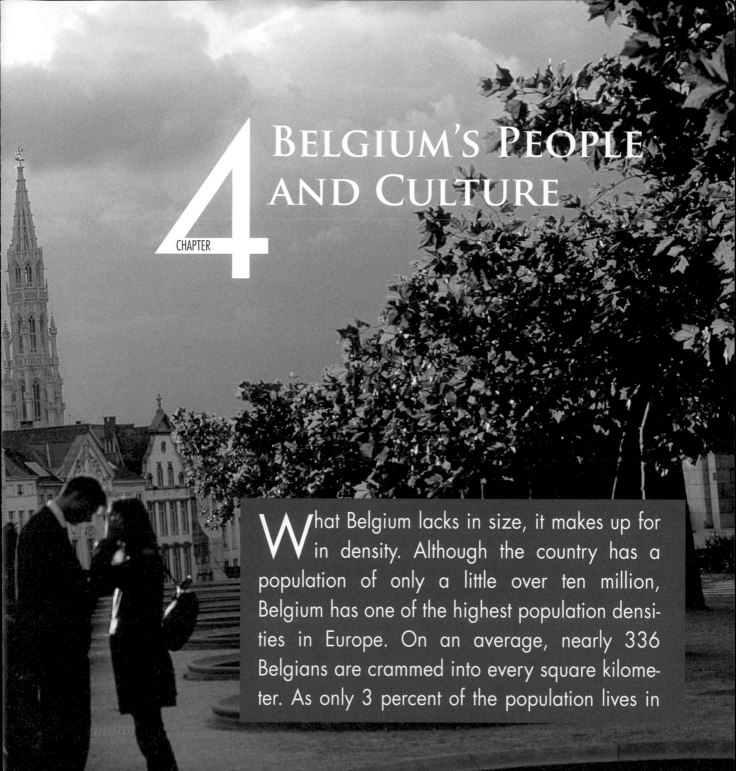

4 BELGIUM'S PEOPLE AND CULTURE

CHAPTER

What Belgium lacks in size, it makes up for in density. Although the country has a population of only a little over ten million, Belgium has one of the highest population densities in Europe. On an average, nearly 336 Belgians are crammed into every square kilometer. As only 3 percent of the population lives in rural areas, population density varies from a scant 140 persons per square mile on the Ardennes plateau to 15,300 per square mile in the Brussels-Capital region.

The Two Faces of Belgium

Belgians have a quirky sense of humor and an appetite for life. Yet, the **bonhomie** of everyday Belgian life conceals a country that is fractured into two linguistic communities. The Dutch-speaking Flemings live in Flanders in the north, and the French-speaking Walloons live in Wallonia in the south. Caught in this deep language divide is the officially **bilingual** capital city of Brussels.

The bitter ethnic tensions between these two communities has ensured that today, Belgium is less of a country than an administrative entity: the French- and Flemish-speaking regions survive as virtually two federal states.

The Flemings are the dominant community in Belgium. They make up nearly 60 percent of the region's population and hold most of the nation's wealth. The Flemings are **industrious**, honest, and cultured people who are not showy or vulgar.

The Walloons make up just over 30 percent of the Belgian population. Although the Walloons once controlled Belgium's coal mines and industries, their economic prosperity declined with the closure of the mines. Proud of their past, and somewhat defensive of their present, Walloons are liberal minded, sociable, and good-natured.

Belgium also has a tiny German-speaking community living in the areas bordering Germany in the east. In Wallonia, three additional regional languages are officially recognized—Champenois, Gaumais, and Picard.

Religion: Looking to Rome

Religion was one of the reasons that Catholic Belgium broke away from the Protestant north of the United Kingdom of the Netherlands in 1830. Today, more than 70 percent of Belgians are Roman Catholic. Islam, Protestantism, and Judaism are other religions widely practiced in Belgium. Many **brotherhoods** and secret societies were also established in Belgium in the mid-twentieth century.

Food and Drink: Chocolates and Beer

To put it mildly, Belgians' appetite for life arches across the language divide. Chocolate is the country's most recognized export. Traditional Belgian chocolates, known as pralines, are filled with cream, liqueurs, nuts, or **ganache**, and are considered by many the best in the world.

As for daily fare, Belgium's two linguistic regions are reflected in the country's cuisine. Fish and **crustaceans** are prominent in Flemish cuisine, reflecting the Dutch influence on the Flemish. Walloon cuisine tends to be more substantial, more spicy, and have more calories than either Flemish or modern French cuisine.

Belgian treats.

QUICK FACTS: THE PEOPLE OF BELGIUM

Population: 10,438,353 (July 2012 est.)
Ethnic Groups: Fleming 58%, Walloon 31%, mixed or other 11%
Age Structure:
0-14 years: 15.9%
15-64 years: 66.1%
65 years and over: 18% (2011 est.)
Population Growth Rate: 0.061% (2012 est.)
Birth Rate: 10.03 births/1,000 population (2012 est.)
Death Rate: 10.63 deaths/1,000 population (July 2012 est.)
Migration Rate: 1.22 migrant(s)/1,000 population (2012 est.)
Infant Mortality Rate: 4.28 deaths/1,000 live births
Life Expectancy at Birth:
Total Population: 79.65 years
Male: 76.49 years
Female: 82.95 years (2012 est.)
Total Fertility Rate: 1.65 children born/woman (2012 est.)
Religions: Roman Catholic 75%, other (includes Protestant) 25%
Languages: Dutch (official) 60%, French (official) 40%, German (official) less than 1%, legally bilingual (Dutch and French)
Literacy Rate: 99%

Note: All figures are from 2011 unless otherwise noted.
Source: www.cia.gov, 2012.

Beer can rightly be called the Belgian national drink, even though Belgians rank fifth as consumers of beer in Europe. Until 1900, every village had its own brewery, with more than three thousand in Wallonia alone. Today, there are 130 breweries in Belgium. Together, they brew more than four hundred varieties of beer.

EDUCATION: A VERY INTENSIVE SYSTEM

Over 99 percent of the adult population in Belgium can read and write. Education is obligatory from age six until eighteen, but most Belgian young adults continue studying until they are twenty-three years old. This makes Belgium's education system the second most intensive in Europe. (The United Kingdom's is even more demanding.) Belgium has an educational system composed of two parts: state **_secular_** schools and private **_denominational_** (mostly Roman Catholic) schools. Both kinds of school are given similar financial assistance by the government. Belgium has several universities as well as other specialized institutions of higher education.

Belgians enjoy gathering at open-air cafés.

SPORTS: A PASSION FOR CYCLING

Sports often makes Belgians put their linguistic *chauvinism* aside and join together. A national passion for cycling has produced Belgium's greatest sportsman to date. Racing cyclist Eddy Merckx won the Tour de France five times, as well as more than 140 other major titles. Auto racing driver Jacky Ickx won eight Formula One Grand Prix races.

A painting by Belgium's Pieter Brueghel the Elder

Soccer is also a popular sport. Although Belgium has never won any major international competition, such as the World Cup or European Championships, it stands a respectable twenty-fourth in the rankings for world soccer.

Recently, tennis has turned the world's gaze to Belgium. In 2004, Justine Henin-Hardenne and Kim Clijsters won a series of tennis grand slam events. Athletes like these are helping to build Belgium's reputation for first-class athletes.

FESTIVALS: CELEBRATIONS GALORE

Belgians love to celebrate. Along with the major religious festivals, Belgians celebrate their country's independence on National Day, July 21. Some of Belgium's biggest festivals revolve around Christian events, even though Christmas itself is a low-key affair.

Four weeks before Lent, the Walloon town of Binche hosts a Carnival, featuring gilles, or clownlike figures. In Flanders, the most important religious festival is the Procession of the Holy Blood, in Brugge. The procession centers on a precious religious relic, a crystal vial supposedly containing the blood of Christ.

Across Belgium, small towns and large cities boast some rather **unorthodox** celebrations, giving further proof that Belgians will create reasons to celebrate if none can be found. Striking examples are the Cat's Festival in Ypres, the Windmill Festival in Lembeke, the Witches' Procession in Nieuwpoort, and the Peasants' Festival in Turnhout.

ART AND ARCHITECTURE

Flemish art flowered during the **Renaissance** of the fifteenth century. The leading painter of the time, Jan Van Eyck, perfected the technique of oil painting and is considered by many art historians to be the first successful painter working in oils. Within the next hundred years, a distinct Flemish style developed, led by Pieter Brueghel the Elder and his two sons, Pieter Brueghel the Younger and Jan Brueghel the Elder. Pieter Brueghel was famous for placing classical or religious events in the contemporary setting of a Flemish village.

Belgium's next great artist was Peter Paul Reubens (1577–1640), one of Europe's greatest artists of the **baroque** period. Among his many paintings is the ceiling of the Banqueting House in London's Whitehall. He was also among the artists who produced designs for tapestries. From the fifteenth to the eighteenth century, Flanders led the world in the production of tapestries.

In the twentieth century, the **surrealist** movement produced an explosion of striking and **subversive** images that reflected the **avant-garde**'s desire to scandalize and unsettle. Rene Magritte and Paul Delvaux were among the leading artists of surrealism.

The architecture of Belgium's cities reflects the country's history as the melting pot of Europe. Traces of Austrian, Spanish, French, and Dutch influences can be seen throughout the country. Perhaps the greatest Belgian architect is Victor Horta, whose Tassel House is the "earliest monument of art nouveau."

Joggers in Bois de la Cambre, a large park in Brussels.

MUSIC

Dutch and French traditions strongly influenced Belgian folk music, with wind and percussion instruments giving energetic company to the accordion. Belgium has also nurtured the talents of some world-class violinists, including Arthur Grumiaux, Eugene Ysaye, Henri Vieutemps, and Charles Auguste de Beriot.

Jazz music has Belgium to thank for its most popular instrument. Belgian Adolphe Sax invented the saxophone in 1845. Using the stage name Johnny Halliday, Belgian Jean-Philippe Smets became France's equivalent of Elvis Presley.

LITERATURE

Belgium has produced one of the most popular writers of the twentieth century. Georges Simenon, creator of Inspector Maigret, published over three hundred novels, mainly on crime subjects. To date, more than 500 million copies of his books have been sold, making Simenon one of the most widely read authors in the world. His books have been translated in many languages and have been adapted for film and television.

One of the most famous Belgian literary figures is not an author at all. Inspector Hercule Poirot appeared in thirty-three novels and sixty-five short stories by British author Agatha Christie. Many of the tales were adapted for film and television. When other characters asked the rotund detective if he were French, he took much delight in telling them he was Belgian. After the much-beloved character died in the book *Curtain* (1975), Hercule Poirot became the only fictional character honored with an obituary on the front page of the New York Times.

Georges Remi (who took the **pen name** Herge) drew the adventures of Tintin. Beginning as a newspaper cartoon, these stories have now sold over 140 million copies in book form. They have been translated into all the major languages of the world and have been made into a major movie.

Joining Remi is a **plethora** of noted Belgian cartoonists including Andre Franquin, Pierre Gulliford, and Jean Roba. Brussels is home to the Belgium Comic Strip Museum.

WHAT WILL THE FUTURE HOLD?

CHAPTER 5

As 2011 began, people around the world were starting to wonder if Belgium has a future as a nation. Six months after the last general election, Belgium still had no new official government in place.

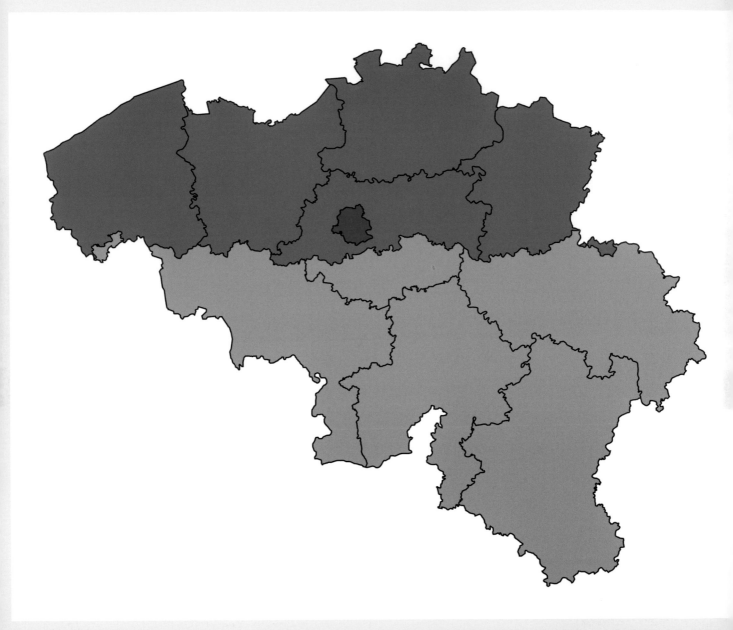

Internal conflicts between the northern region, Flanders, and the southern region, Wallonia, causes political chaos which threatens to tear Belgium apart.

The royal palace in Brussels, Belgium.

Meanwhile, the Flemish **nationalist** Bart De Wever, head of the country's largest political party, wanted to split Belgium into two states. In an interview with the newspaper *Spiegel* that caused a scandal in his country, he claimed his nation had "no future."

Belgium had sunk into political chaos. The country was divided into two camps that opposed each other and were unable to find common ground: the **socialists**, who won the most votes in Wallonia, the French-speaking southern region of the country; and the nationalist **conservatives** in Flanders, the wealthier Dutch-speaking northern region.

In the interview, De Wever described Belgium as the "sick man" of Europe. The interview caused a huge outcry throughout Belgium. The French-speaking daily newspaper *Le Soir* called it "a bomb" meant to stir up the markets for Belgian government bonds. The Flemish newspapers were more sympathetic but they criticized the timing of the interview. De Wever himself said he regretted

The Belgian flag.

if anybody felt insulted, but he insisted, "My analysis is accurate. There is nothing in the interview that is not true." He said that the monarchy, one of the only forces that holds Belgium together, is a romantic holdover from the past that benefits only the Walloons and not the Flemish.

Not everyone agreed with De Wever, however. Herman Van Rompuy, a former Belgian premier who went on later to be president of the Council of the European Union, insisted that Belgium's future was strong, despite its current problems. "The economic fundamentals of Belgium are healthier than people believe," he told *Le Soir* in December 2010. "The next government will have to do some reforms, but we don't have major problems for the moment."

Throughout the crisis, a caretaker government led by the outgoing prime minister managed Belgium. Finally, in December of 2011, prime minister Elio di Rupo was sworn in. At the same time, Belgium managed to make a success of its six-month stint at the EU presidency, which ended on December 31, 2010. Some political experts claimed this proved that the country is more than capable of surviving.

Not everyone feels so hopeful. Many wonder if Belgium's political crisis is just the beginning of a final showdown that will bring an end to the nation forever. If that should happen, the EU would help provide much-needed stability for both the Flemish and the Walloons.

Nobody knows for sure what will happen. Only the future will tell!

TIME LINE

1st Millennium BCE	Celtic tribes, such as the Belgae, settle in Western Europe.
58 BCE	The Belgae fight with Julius Caesar's forces and surrender.
3rd–5th centuries CE	The Franks settle in Gaul. Christianity spreads.
800 CE	Frank King Charlemagne is crowned Emperor of the Romans in Rome.
1308	Henry VII of Luxembourg becomes the German emperor and is crowned Henry IV.
1369	Margaret, the daughter of the last count of Flanders, marries Phillip the Bold of Burgundy. Flanders comes under Burgundian rule.
15th century	Dukes of Burgundy win control of what is now Belgium.
1477	Mary, daughter and heiress of the last Duke of Burgundy marries Maximilian of Austria; Belgium comes under the power of the Habsburg dynasty.
1500	Future German emperor Charles V, grandson of Maximilian, is born in Ghent.
1531	Brussels becomes the capital of the Spanish Netherlands.
1555	Charles V turns the Spanish Netherlands over to his son Phillip II; Spain starts a reign of terror against Protestants.
1579	The seven, mainly Protestant northern provinces join to form the independent nation of Netherlands.
1648	Treaty of Westphalia; Spain recognizes the independence of Netherlands.
1701–1714	Spanish War of Succession; Belgium and Luxembourg pass under the authority of the Holy Roman Emperor Charles VI and his Habsburg successors.

1795	France, under Napoleon Bonaparte, annexes Belgium and Luxembourg.
1815	Battle of Waterloo; Holland and Belgium form the Kingdom of the Netherlands under William I of Orange.
1830–1831	Revolution in Brussels; Catholic Belgium breaks away from Protestant Netherlands.
1831	Leopold of Saxe-Coburg becomes first Belgian king.
1914–1918	During World War I, German troops invade Belgium and Luxembourg.
1940–1944	During World War II, German troops invade Belgium. Belgium is set free in 1944.
1951	King Baudouin I ascends the throne.
1957	Belgium joins the European Economic Community (now the European Union), and Brussels becomes the headquarters of the European Community.
1959	Constitutional reform gives both linguistic groups (Flemish and French) more autonomy in economic and cultural matters.
1993	King Baudouin I dies and is replaced by his brother, King Albert II.
January 2002	Euro replaces the Belgian franc.
July 2003	European Convention meets in Brussels to draft the Constitution of the European Union.
June 2004	The Constitution of the European Union is adopted.
2007	Belgium enters a political crisis between the Flemish- and Walloon-backed parties.
2008	Belgium faces a serious economic crisis.
2010	The general election fails to elect a new government, and a caretaker government takes over while Belgium's arguing political parties try to find a resolution. Belgium serves as president of the EU.
2011	Elio di Rupo becomes prime minister

FIND OUT MORE

IN BOOKS

Burgan, Michael. *Belgium*. New York: Scholastic Library Publishing, 2000.
Claus, Hugo. *The Sorrow of Belgium*. New York: Penguin, 2003.
Jockel, Nils. *Pieter Bruegel's Tower of Babel*. New York: Prestel Publishing, 1998.
Venezia, Mike. *Rene Magritte (Getting to Know the World's Greatest Art)*. New York: Scholastic
   Library Publishing, 2003.

ON THE INTERNET

Travel Information
www.belgium-tourism.com
www.lonelyplanet.com/destinations/europe/belgium/
www.trabel.com
www.visitbelgium.com

History and Geography
www.geographia.com/belgium
www.mapzones.com/world/europe/belgium/historyindex.php

Economic and Political Information
www.belgium.be
www.cia.gov/cia/publications/factbook/geos/be.html
www.nationmaster.com/country/be/Government

Culture and Festivals
www.ricksteves.com/plan/festivals/benfest.htm

Publisher's note:
The websites listed on this page were active at the time of publication. The publisher is not responsible
for websites that have changed their addresses or discontinued operation since the date of publication. The publisher will review and update the website list upon each reprint.

GLOSSARY

abdicated: Resigned a position.

austerity: A saving economy, or act of self-denial.

autonomous: Able to act independently.

autonomy: Independence.

avant-garde: Artistic movement whose works are innovative, experimental, or unconventional.

baroque: A highly ornamental seventeenth-century art style.

bicameral: A form of government consisting of two separate and distinct lawmaking assemblies.

bilingual: The ability to speak two languages.

bonhomie: Easy, good-natured friendliness.

boycott: A refusal to buy a certain product in order to achieve a particular political goal.

brotherhoods: Organizations of men united for a common purpose.

Celtic: Pertaining to an ancient Indo-European people who lived in central and western Europe in pre-Roman times.

chauvinism: An aggressive patriotism or sense of superiority.

civil war: A conflict between citizens of the same country.

collective security: Safety that depends on countries working together.

colonial: In this context, the desire to establish colonies in other lands.

confederation: A group of loosely aligned states or countries.

conglomeration: A mass of dissimilar elements.

coniservative: People who are cautious about change and hold on to traditional values.

constitutional monarchy: A system of government where a king or queen's power is limited by a constitution that protects citizens' rights.

crustaceans: Hard-shelled sea creatures with several pairs of jointed legs, two pairs of antennae, and eyes at the ends of stalks.

deficits: To spend more than earned.

denominational: Relating to a religious grouping within a faith.

depleted: Used up.

duchy: A territory ruled over by a duke or duchess.

exiled: Cast out; forced to leave one's country.

flax: Plants whose flowers produce seeds from which linseed oil is produced, and whose stalks are used to obtain the fiber to make linen.

ganache: A rich chocolate filling or sauce used for cakes and pastries.

gross domestic product (GDP): The total value of all goods and services produced within a country in a year, minus the amount it spent in other countries.

hydroelectric: Generated by water power.

industrious: Hardworking.

integration: Unity; the act of becoming one thing.

mechanized: Made dependent on machines.

nationalists: People who feel very proud of their country.

neutral: Impartial.

parliamentary: A system of government where the executive power is vested in a cabinet composed of members of the legislature who are individually and collectively responsible to the legislature.

pen name: A false name taken by an author.

plethora: A large amount of something.

refineries: Places where substances such as oil or sugar are processed.

Renaissance: The period in European history from the fourteenth through the sixteenth centuries in which the Middle Ages ended and major cultural and artistic changes took place.

Resistance: A secret, illegal organization that fights for national freedom against an occupying power.

right-wing: Conservative.

secede: Drop out of a country.

secular: Not controlled by a religious body.

service industries: Business that provide services for people (such as hospitals, restaurants, etc.).

socialists: People who believe that the government should control the economy.

sovereign: Self-governing and independent.

subversive: Intended to undermine or overthrow a government or institution.

suppressed: Put down by authority or force.

surrealist: Someone who followed the early 20th-century art and literary movement that tried to represent the unconscious mind by creating fantastic imagery and placing elements together that did not seem to belong together.

thermal: Created by heat.

unorthodox: Not following traditional beliefs or practices.

volatile: Easily upset or excited.

zenith: The highest point of something.

INDEX

PICTURE CREDITS

About the Authors and the Consultant

Authors

Ida Walker is a graduate of the University of Northern Iowa and did graduate work in Museum Studies/Art History at Syracuse University. She enjoys studying the history and cultures of other countries.

Shaina Carmel Indovino is a writer and illustrator living in Nesconset, New York. She graduated from Binghamton University, where she received degrees in sociology and English. Shaina has enjoyed the opportunity to apply both of her fields of study to her writing and she hopes readers will benefit from taking a look at the countries of the world through more than one perspective.

Series Consultant

Ambassador John Bruton served as Irish Prime Minister from 1994 until 1997. As prime minister, he helped turn Ireland's economy into one of the fastest-growing in the world. He was also involved in the Northern Ireland Peace Process, which led to the 1998 Good Friday Agreement. During his tenure as Ireland's prime minister, he also presided over the European Union presidency in 1996 and helped finalize the Stability and Growth Pact, which governs management of the euro. Before being named the European Commission Head of Delegation in the United States, he was a member of the convention that drafted the European Constitution, signed October 29, 2004.

The European Commission Delegation to the United States represents the interests of the European Union as a whole, much as ambassadors represent their countries' interests to the U.S. government. Matters coming under European Commission authority are negotiated between the commission and the U.S. administration.